Jesus Isn't Coming Back

Jesus Isn't Coming Back

They Sent Me Instead

Kaya Gibson

Rhonda Gibson
Jesus Isn't Coming Back

Published by Spines

ISBN: 979-8-89569-412-1

Contents

Introduction

Welcome, and thank you for coming to read the next pages of the journey of:

My life which is primarily about you. I want to thank all of you who began this journey with me when you read my first book, "Released." I thank you for your positive and beautiful responses, especially those of you who made it a point to thank me for coming back. These pages will tell you more about why I came and what I've been commissioned by Source to expose, explain, and do to create peace and paradise on Earth. The catch is I carry the knowledge and channel of the knower. Yet, you are the body of humankind, and you, as we all, are being given the choice: to recognize the reality of your state of being, make the corrections, and do good, or continue in vanity and self-destruct. However, should you choose self-destruction, you will go alone, for the earth is the living, and we shall go forward in peace, joy, health, and happiness as it should have been from the beginning.

I began with a few quotes that may resonate with you as they do with me, and it will be evident as to why, as you hear and as I have heard from the authentic intelligence of the "SOURCE" that is our manifester, our creator, our vibration, frequency, our energy being within. It is known as love/goodness, the greatest power, the only authentic power in our existence.

A special acknowledgment to our ancestors, the ancients, and those who live within: I have received Malcolm, Martin, Meager, Fannie Lou, Shirley Chisholm, Harriet Tubman, Sojourner Truth, Coretta, Thurgood Marshall, Tupac, Eartha, Michael, and so many more great cloud of witnesses, whose voices continue in my heart and head, guiding me to my destiny, for they know that their lives, nor mine, have not been in vain.

Quotes:

"**In this age of Technological Inhumanity, Scientific Atrocity, Atomic mis-philosophy, Nuclear mis-energy, it's a world that Forces lifelong insecurity.**"

— **Bob Marley.**

"**What life has taught me, I want to share with those who want to learn.**
There is one human race with many cultures.
Until the philosophy that holds one Culture superior and another inferior is finally and permanently! Discredited! and Abandoned! THERE WILL BE WAR!

Until there are no longer first-class and second-class citizens of any nation! THERE WILL BE WAR!

Until the color of a human's skin is of no more significant than the color of their eyes! THERE WILL BE WAR!

Until basic human rights are equally guaranteed to all without regard to culture! THERE WILL BE WAR!

Until that day, The Dream of Lasting Peace, World Citizenship, and the Rule of INTERNATIONAL MORALITY will REMAIN a fleeting illusion to be pursued and never attained."

EVERYWHERE IS WAR. IU.M. Haile Selassie 1, i

" Every Gun that is Made, Every Warship launched, and Every Rocket Fired signifies, in the final sense, a Theft from those who hunger and are not fed, those who are cold and are not clothed. This world in arms is not spending money alone. It is spending the sweat of its Laborers, the genius of its Scientists, the hopes of its Children. This is not a way of life at all in any true sense. Under the clouds of war, humanity is hanging on a CROSS of iron.

D. Eisenhower April 16,1953... $10 Billion a month.

To announce that, there must be no criticism. Of the President, or that we stand by the "President, right or wrong," is not only unpatriotic. "And servile, but it is morally treasonable to the American public."

— Theodore Roosevelt, 1918

"WAKE UP AND LIKE, MARLEY"

Life is one big road with lots of signs. When you're running through the ruts, don't you complicate your mind, flee from hate, mischief and jealousy, don't bury your faith, and put your dreams to reality? Rise, you mighty people. There is work to be done, so let's do it little by little. Rise from your sleepless slumber where more than the sands of the seashore were more than number altogether. Wake up and live now. Wake up...

"So much trouble in the world. Bless my eyes. This morning, Ma's sun is on the rise once again. The way earthly things are going, anything can happen. You see men sailing on their EGO trips, blasting off on their space-ships, a million miles from reality, no care for you, no care for me; now we're sitting on a time bomb. I know the time has come. What goes on up is coming on down. What goes around, it comes around."

I "Declaration of Independence"

When, in the Course of human events, it becomes necessary for one people to DISSOLVE the POLITICAL bands which have connected them with another and to assume among the powers of the earth the separate and equal station to which the Laws of Nature and of Nature's God entitle them, a decent respect to the opinions of humankind requires that they should declare the causes which impel them to the separation.

We hold these truths to be self-evident: that all HU means are created equal, that they are endowed by their Creator with certain UNALIENABLE Rights, and that among these are Life, Liberty, and the pursuit of Happiness. — That to secure these rights, Governments are instituted among Men. DERIVING their just powers from the CONSENT of the governed, — That WHEN-

EVER any Form of Government becomes DESTRUC-TIVE of these ends, it is the RIGHT of the People to alter or to ABOLISH it, and to INSTITUTE new Government, laying its foundation on such principles and organizing its powers in such form, as to them shall seem most likely to effect {their Safety and Happiness. Prudence, indeed, will dictate that Governments long established should not be changed for light and transient causes; and accordingly, all experience hath shown that mankind is more disposed to suffer, while evils are sufferable than to right themselves by abolishing the forms to which they are accustomed. But WHEN A LONG TRAIN of abuses and usurpations, pursuing invariably the same Object, EVINCES a DESIGN to reduce them under absolute Despotism, it is their RIGHT, it is their DUTY, to throw off such Government and to provide new Guards for their future security, j- Such has been the patient sufferance of these Colonies. Such is now the necessity which constrains them to alter their former System.

Morton White writes of the American revolutionaries, "The notion that they had a duty to rebel is extremely important to stress, for it shows that they thought they were complying with the commands of natural law and of nature's God when they threw off absolute despotism ." The U.S. Declaration of Independence states that when a long train of abuses and usurpations, pursuing invariably the same Object, evinces a design to reduce them under absolute Despotism, It is their right, it is their duty to throw off such Government (emphasis added) The phrase long train of abuses" is a reference to John Locke's similar statement in Second Treatise of Government, where he explicitly established the overthrow of a tyrant as an obligation. Martin Luther King likewise held the duty of the people to resist unjust law.

About the Author
A LITTLE BIT ABOUT ME

Priestess Seifuala Adnorhijah Kaya

Seifuala means "words of truth," Adnorhijah means "one sent of love," and KAYA means Strong root healing of the nations."

Author/Producer:

- "RELEASED" by Kaya Gibson (amazon.com)
- "Thrilled to Life" Spoken Word CD:
- "Deux Ex Machina: Divine Intervention" Reggae Music CD
- "A Divine Intervention," music theater, KC Fringe 2013.

- S.I.N Political StringsKcFringe2015
- Spiritual Counselor, Lyricist, Singer/Songwriter.
- Poetess, educator, motivational speaker,
- "Human Rights Peace Activist"
- "Ambassador for the United Trade Council,
- unifiedexchange.org [unifiedexchange.org]
- Former teacher KCMO SD,
- Member of Delta Sigma Theta
- Sorority Epsilon Psi '78, KC Alumni Chapter
- Exec, producer, host; Reggae, Culture, Rising cable,
- music/video show, '93
- DJ: "Culture Exchange" radio show88[f], KKFI,
- Mo State Coordinator for "Million Woman March" '97,
- The Federal Democratic Republic of Ethiopia Abroad. Chaplain
- Presidents 6/Local 22,
- Philanthropist.

TRAVEL Performances

Festivals, Clubs, Colleges, Hotels, Coffeehouses etc, Kansas City surrounding areas, Saint Louis, New York, Oakland, Louisiana, Tel Aviv, Jerusalem, Cairo, Athens,

Montego Bay. Israel, Turkey, Greece, Egypt, performances from bus stops in Cairo, through the trench town of Jamaica, at many festivals, including KC Spirit Fest, the heart of America Jam Fest., American rights festival, Hemp Fest. Her original combination of reggae hip hop rock is riveting, righteous and refreshing!

Sahj *KAYA likens herself to a flint stone; a piece of flint creates a spark that grows a great fire of awareness, consciousness and enlightenment... I am inspired by love; it is the most powerful energy on the earth. It is the author of our creation. I've always loved to sing and have sung in talent shows and choirs.

In 1983, after hearing Bob Marley for the first time, I was more than inspired. I felt an immediate spiritual connection. It was music that felt good, with an infectious sound and a profound message for the mind, body, and spirit. Stevie Wonder, Marvin Gaye, Michael Jackson, Earth, Wind & Fire have all had a great influence on me as an artist because of their enlightening, insightful lyrics and varied musical expressions.

The message I want people to get from my gifts is that we can break the human cycles of pain, that it's the last days of the old ways, that the media is deceiving you, that the Tower of the bible is a tower of libel. Still, love, the greatest power in the world, is traveling a long way, looking for a place to stay, that we got to work together and make it a Family of humanity. Whether we thrive, survive, perish, or die, the power and choice lie within I+I US, JE+US, WE, in our human hands.

Part One

Chapter 1

Self Inflicted Nonsense (S.I.N.) &
Political Strings

Why do you think and accept it is normal for guns to exist, a God-given right? What God gives you the right to kill and also says thou shall not kill? Hypocritical, to say the least, nonsensical at best. Have I got news for you? The children shall lead them to uncover and reveal the great deception that has held the world hostage at the tyranny of men and those who aid them in maintaining and sustaining the inequities of life.

BY THE CONSENT of THE PEOPLE

The Government to rule, the police to protect, and all that it rules have become the oppressors of I. I + US, daily crucifying JE (I) S (I) US, the body of humanity, provoking and tempting the love energy of the Christ that dwells in the body of humanity to turn to hate, vengeance and violence in reaction to the insidious nonstop as the preamble again refers to the train of offenses, it simulates and stimulates war with others putting our families in harm's way and neglect and disregard their sacrifice. Make Excuses for its behaviors and justify itself by paying voluntary/mandatory taxes. Abuse and neglect are what we, the people, get for paying their checks. They have started many a war, slipping bombs and bullets through the back door. Counterfeit burning bush falsely accused U. The murder your poor. Do the police protect you, or do they make you sweat and feel threatened? Intimidation distress, so you pay their check, and they make you sweat. Thinking about thing

What I know

The Liar has blinded your eyes, filling you with despise for yourself. He has tried in every way to make a slave of you for him. The trickery is on you through a tool of vanity that feeds the appetite of the ego.

There is no such thing as death.

There is neither male nor female; there are humans, there are humans with wombs, and there are humans without wombs who have been categorized and labeled to add to the confusion of your existence.

There is no God that gave anyone the authority to

create tools to murder, weapons to kill, then steal, and then destroy, like the civilizations that exhibited a culture and existence without war or weapons of war among humans. The traditions and the ways of "men" have made the commandment of love non-affect. These traditions were created by men and sown through his story through religion.

Humans are created through source. The source is energy vibrations frequencies distributed and compounded in different consistencies, creating and manifesting all that we see, hear, and feel. There is the source whose authentic pure energy disburses and reception the equilibrium balance, producing what is good energy. This is the universal consistency that is also called love, which is the manifestation of the energy that resides in the anatomical biologically designed for the good. I love the humane energy to have a form that could sustain and thrive in that was also compatible with the environment it would thrive and enjoy. NOW, the spirit energy of good of humanness also had a compatible vessel to matriculate with comfort and pleasure. The human was made as one.

They had initially identified by as some as hermaphrodites, then as part of a compliment, one was designed with a womb and an inside manufacturing reproduction center to prepare a suit for another spirit being to enjoy what was called earth, known as the heart of the universe and through the human with a "womb" came the human without a womb, one that was wombless. Through the human that was without a womb came jealousy, envy, fear, hate, deception, destruction, pain and death. There is the human with a womb, and the wombless human is raised as equal partners. The wombless human, out of fear and jealousy, removed itself from the partnership inequality to devise the great deception and take all the power it saw in the human with a womb and all that it was able to produce from its womb; it removed itself to challenge and defeat subdue and enslave the human with a womb and all that it reproduced through deceit trickery mental, verbal physical assault intimidation and fear. Removing itself from humankind labeled it self-mankind, which was no man at all, no kindness, no humaneness, no kind of man at all. The first rebellion against goodness source energy power, taking the good energy called good energy that had no good in it. Mankind created, manufactured and distributed a good concept and narrative to emotionally and spiritually enslave humans with a womb through the war tool of religion, fear and deception. This is the beginning of the history of mankind that, through the creation of a manmade concept of a god whose power was through fear, was recognized as a man giving so-called me the authority over life and death. Who created genders, labels, categories and every and any means to create and maintain separation, division, conflict, negative competition, jealousies, and differences to secure its power of DIVIDE

AND CONQUER, the only true weapon that has succeeded thus far, humans, have to be made aware that when they were created their spirit being is hundred percent 'feminine' hundred percent masculine equal. Developed correctly, each a nurturer, and each has all the qualities that represent a humanely balanced human being until they were separated and identified in categories that created false labeling and narrative for hierarchical status; humans with wombs shall be labeled a woman, one weaker than a wombless man and inferior and all else to follow suit from birth to death.

At the beginning of his story was the word spell, the lie created to deceive the world, and the word was God, a man-made concept, EGO-based, a God with a man's face on it and no good in it. To subdue and destroy all! That is good for a God of ego, and through history and evil deeds, blood runs 6 feet deep over the earth with famine in fruitfulness and droughts in floods; this is the evidence of his evil against its creator; all that is good and himself, "God repented that he made man" (the God concept and the war against the creator good/love and himself.

1. God is a man-made concept."
2. Religion is a man-made concept to support and uphold the man-made concept of an idle/idol energy God for humans to be entrapped and enslaved by praying to and waiting on something that doesn't exist.

Religion, the tradition of men, has divided the body of the world to create chaos, conflict, and competition to maintain control of humanity through lies and deceit, teaching that the god of this world is "white supremacy," introduced and covered by the whitewash of religion.

The great DECEPTION is that there is a God that looks like a man and is in control of all things, the big lie of the liar that bases very else that this liar does on this lie and for anyone to challenge it;.. the fury of the greatest peer pressure of all rains down, however, the rain is dried by the Sun, the truth that lights the way.

There is no death; all are transitions.

The abominable acts that take place on this earth are created and carried out by "men" and those others who aid them in their wickedness and distortion of life.

This was so eloquently channeled through me from NEDA: "Tears of Blood."

There is no justification for the existence of war.

Just as one who has been brought into the world has the right to choose to live this life, one also has a choice not to.

Kids are labeled as the offspring of the so-called goat, which is defined as an animal, and these labels transfer onto the child, which is the offspring of a human being, which is the reproduction of the divine feminine divine masculine is induced and developed in animal behavior emphasis on physical emotion lacking spiritual balance. Continuous conflict butting heads, lack of discipline, aggressive territorial. It said to train up a child.

Jesus did not come to save you from your self-inflicted nonsense, SIN. He came as the presence of the divine masculine to exhibit how the divine masculine lives. In love, truth, righteousness, integrity, balanced emulating the good in humanness, in humanity love, creativity, life, gratitude, and humility also exposed the indignity in humanity imposed and enforced on humankind, just as you all are carriers of that DNA.

And just like you, he was murdered and was made an example of whoever would stand for the divine, for he that is the liar has said there is none good but god. I know there is no god, but there is good. They say God is love, but when God is called your pen, there is no love. Love exists omnipotent and ever-present; god is a man-made religion to deceive the world. The biggest emperor wears no clothes scheme of all time! It is Love. Call it call; if it's a dog, call it, it will call it god, and a man appears to assume authority over others that he has given to himself by himself supported by them like himself and others that have been seduced, intimidated or by worldwide religious peer pressure.

So if your god is who you say "he" is, why do you need guns or bombs to resolve any conflict? Why do you behave as If killing, murdering, and slaughter are ever justified? Why does it exist? It is by design.

"Yes, the great deception, hiding you from you in plain sight yet unable to see yourself by the gospel spell you are under. Break the spell; the blinders fall off."

JE French means I. S making the I plural, I's =US JE+S=us is a code word, it is a body of individuals that carry the divine feminine and divine masculine's DNA spirit of love truth creative healing power identified as Christ:

Yes, "JESUS CHRIST" (code word) is you, yet cruci-fied, not resurrected. The body is resurrected by the removal of the slave block of ignorance, the gospel spell of white supremacy, and human indignity. Who am I to make such claims and assertions? I will let the one who sent me introduce me. As I have surrendered myself for good, for love of truth revealing and channeling divine source.

Chapter 2

The Message to the Human With a Womb From the Mother of the Universe

66 And a voice from heaven said, "This is My beloved Sun, in whom I am well pleased!"

This vessel has submitted her life so that I may matriculate upon the earth for a brief period to reveal and establish healing and balance to Earth. She has been on watchman's duty. Now the time has come, for sudden destruction has entered the minds of the womb-less (hu)man to kill, steal, and destroy Precious Mother Earth and its inhabitants. MA Sun,

Seifuala Adnorhijah Kaya's words of truth, one sent of love, strong root healing of the nations..(SahjKaya) _

First, I am to address the humans with a womb of the World, all of you human beings who have a womb in your body, all who were born with a womb, all who have brought a human being into this earth, into this world. Listen, it is you who must hear; it is you who have been prepared to save Mother Earth. Know that the Mother, the nurturer of the Universe, who has sprinkled life throughout, has this word for you.

This message to you has come because the travail of your weeping has been reverberating through the universal council chambers of the nurturers, our SUNs. This we refer to all that is given life through the family of life, of humanity.

This message to you is to assure you that you're weeping, and that of the humans that you bore and the ones that do not want to come to this place, earth, that was given to be made into paradise but has become the utter human desecration and destruction HAS BEEN HEARD. It is time to

This vessel has submitted her life so that I may matriculate upon the Earth for a brief period to reveal and establish healing and balance to the Earth.

She has been on watchman's duty. Now, the time has come for sudden destruction to enter the minds of the wombless (hu) man, to kill, steal and destroy Precious Mother Earth and its inhabitants. The Womb (hu)Man that has brought human beings into this earth has been prepared to save Mother Earth; she will soon recognize and Know that the Mother of the Universe, who has sprinkled life throughout this world, is present. The travail of weeping has been reverberating through the universal council chambers. These we refer to are all that is given life through the family of life, of humanity.

This message is to assure you that you're weeping, and that of the humans born and the ones that are heard, who do not want to be born to this place, Earth, which was meant to be made into paradise but has become the utter human desecration and destruction.

> "It is time to end this atrocity that has become a stench in the nostrils of MA-Our Mother of the Universe."

The blood/oil of the earth and the blood of humans that burns like the incense of ether have anesthetized the people of the world, poisoning their environment, minds, bodies, and hearts.

In the womb (hu)man beings are the restoration from centuries of deception that led to the deterioration of humanity while dissecting it for selfishness and vanity and abusing all of creation and its inhabitants.

End this atrocity that has become a stench in the nostrils of MA-Our Mother (the nurturer) of the Universe. The blood/oil of the earth, the blood of humans that burns like the incense of ether, has anesthetized the people of the world. It has poisoned their environment, their minds, bodies, and hearts.

In your being, the womb (hu)man is the restoration from centuries of deception that led you to now. Here, the deterioration of humanity occurs while the wombless human is dissecting and abusing all of creation and its inhabitants. There are things that must be done. All that is needed is present in order to begin to "Rebalance the earth, initiating radial healing, now recognizing that this living organism, Earth Mother, is the sustainer of human life and is threatened."

In the beginning, the ancients gave the herbs as the energy resource to sustain humankind upon the earth. Cannabis/Hemp was given as the primary renewable, unlimited, clean energy resource. It does everything that fossil fuels and petroleum do without contaminating the planet. It fulfills all the uses provided by trees. It is a 120-day crop. It grows where there is earth. It needs to be planted over the earth to replace all fossil fuel use, clean the air, and cure the ozone problem. It heals and strengthens all it touches.

ALL fossil fuel drills and pipelines must be removed and end drilling from the body of the earth. The oil from the cellulose and the seeds of the hemp plant, the original energy resource, will replace everything that was made from fossil fuel and petroleum, making them biodegradable and eliminating the need for landfills. It heals and strengthens the topsoil and uses its own natural, nontoxic insecticide and nontoxic insulation. This is the answer for the New World we are commissioned to build. All that we live in today is toxic and must be replaced. One consolation. The building is cleaning the environment for healthy humans and never-ending jobs until paradise has been built so that none will be without an occupation. Now, in the new world that we build, all the money/resources will no longer need to be used for war, death, and destruction but for dismantling the old and building the 'new.' This is the economic restoration through agriculture and nonlethal, nontoxic, unlimited energy sources. This plant was made illegal, illegally by the U.S. misrepresented its character and uses, deceiving the entire world through the United Nations and seducing the nations of the world into a bogus drug war under threat of withholding financial aid when, in fact, it is a war on people, making a plant with no lethal attributes an enemy. It cannot kill you or hurt you; from ancient times until today, there is no record of hurt or harm from use, only unsubstantiated misrepresentation and incredible fabrications/lies of the

U.S. The results of this have been catastrophic for the world. It has created a 21st-century 'legalized' slave trade called the penal industrial complex, being the highest incarceration in the world.

The government /foreign entity that you have allowed to rule over you has become destructive to the well-being of humanity and a threat to communities throughout the universe and the solar system.

The building manufacturing strategic designs for weapons of war must cease and desist on planet Earth. These manufacturing companies must be shut down. All the weapons of war, including guns, must be confiscated, destroyed, and dismantled until there is no one on this planet. The creation of these weapons has indeed "BROKEN THE UNIVERSAL LAW OF LIFE, MASS MURDER OVER THE PLANET IS THE KARMIC RESPONSE" will continue and accelerate. The True transition that is to take place on this earth begins with what you must understand: that you have sacrificed your lives and your children's lives, and the life of the planet has been compromised.

So this final sacrifice that is to be made for this transition that on the day of the day chosen by the Creator, all womb men of the world (unless you choose to end up as LOTS wife turns to stone by nuclear ash), your children and all those you are responsible for, all the womb men of the world that hear MA voice as it echoes throughout the world to the hearts and minds ears of you, the tree of life, the fruit of your womb wake to gather all that you need for at least one week plus. For the 4 days, you must remain in your homes and secure locations; this will be a world-wide Sabbath Celebration for the WOMB MAN. We must agree upon this one thing and do it. This will be the separation of those who choose life. You must not hear or obey any other voice on this day, you must not go to work, and no one is anywhere. There will be people who transition on that day and know they are not dead; there is no death.

"Death is a creation of man, a man-made concept to maintain an illusion of fear to maintain control over the faithless and the fearful to give him an appearance of power. We Must remove those that thrive on greed and destruction and Raise life's renewal paradise production. Human hands created it under tyranny; human hands and hearts shall recreate it through UNITY, JUSTICE, and EQUALITY.

The POWER of life is in the oracle, the whole chalice, the WOMB (hu)man. PREPARE Your STRATEGY TO WITHDRAW FOR YOUR SABBATH (R&R) CELEBRATION!

While "The Beast of War" must be starved to death!

The Unholy Communion is against WOMBMAN and her children and has committed the abomination of desolation and abominable crimes against children. These heinous institutionalized entities must be exposed, dismantled, and dissolved. All things related to their existence must be surrendered to the world court For justice and restitution for all that has been damaged by and because of their existence (why is it that institutions that have been proven with evidence that it has molested, raped, countless amount of children and the people did not and has not risen in outrage at the abomination against children such that they would rise in righteous indignation, shut down and board up these sepulcher of vileness against the innocent Man-made fear and religion are authored by the deceiver, the father of lies. There is no lack of anything that we and our children cannot have, for the blessing, healing, happiness, and all that the human heart desires are in our midst, within our reach, ready to be achieved. The one obstacle is the BLOCK of ignorance, guilt, and shame imposed on your life, making the womb (hu)man to blame by a world government out to kill her and her seed, as it was/is done, written in his story, which led to the creation of hell, bombs, bullets, legalized murders, and jails. Through the womb (hu)man now, Her story we tell for the resurrection of paradise no longer for sale.

We shall raise the "EQUALITARIAN SOCIETY" the WAY it should be: paradise, thy Christ, dom come a new day, a new way where all will be free and live life living and living life happily.

While self-appointed god power spirit of destruction, control and death, the systematic regulated process of extinction of the cultures is blatant, the primary target for the maintenance of control and the police, the arm of restraint for resistance control. We pay their checks and allow this abuse; it's a shame. Are you hearing what you're praying? Are you meaning what you are saying, I'sus Children, Jesus, why is it that while an institution exists from its inception to produce and maintain the great deception, which has been proven with evidence that it has molested and raped countless amounts of children, the people did not and have not risen in outrage at the abomination against children such that the world has never known would rise in righteous indignation to shut down and board up these "whited sepulchers" of vileness against innocence? So why do they continue to support, with tithes and offerings, an entity that is the embodiment of all that is against Christ? It is against the truth and is guilty of the worst crimes known to humankind. Why do you bow to this evil and continue to feed it to your children? Are you afraid? Are you cowards? Do you profess Christ but are afraid of the "devil," whose only power is the power you give it? For we were not given a spirit of fear, but many have adopted it.

In the CHRISTDOM, no blood is shed; in the CHRISTDOM every one is fed by the sun that makes all things grow. In the Christdom, what we know what we live in peace and love, and all is shared; there's much to give; in Christendom, it says there are many mansions, not just a few, and the streets are paved with the reflection of the sun in gold like a hue, earth and humans and all thing are created new... It's the new earth design, the Paradise View...

Chapter 3

"Wombman Empowerment: NEDA Tears of Blood"

" NEDA TEARS OF BLOOD-WOMBMAN EMPOWERMENT THE STANCE MUST BE!

— Written by Rhonda Gibson © 2009
Performed by Seifuala Adnorhijah Kaya
(SahjKaya)

"NEDA, NEDA, NEDA, the sound of your
  name,
So beautiful, so sweet.
Your voice is so strong, cry out to us.
Women empowerment the stance must,
Here we have the Victory.
Mothers' suns take back our dignity.

We live we die for liberty, not for men or
    sons that do not honor me/we, we/me.
Tears rise in my eyes as the people
    demonstrate.
My heart felt the pain. Oh, my tears have
    turned to blood running down my face,
I saw it for a brief moment. Out of body, on
    YouTube
Seeing the disgrace of the human race,
    doing evil to each other, the way that
    they do
In the presence of the Creation, I saw this
    human disgrace through tears of blood
    running down my face. I'm set free
    now, believe it or not! Happy as a bird
    in a tree now, set free from the pain
    and horror you made life out to
    be now
I now know there is no death,
You used fear to keep control of us,
If you claim you didn't make the pain
Who was killed today while bullets still fly
    free?
You stare me in my bloodied face and
    proclaim you care,
How could you? When you MAKE these
    weapons, and you LET them be made.

And turn your face, and you look the
other way. And it ends up in my heart!
What excuses will you make today,
When men are murderers of humans.
They justify killing in the streets.
Killing one another is how men compete.
As your bullet shot through the air into my
heart,
A final image,
You've torn my earth apart, living out a lie!
Honoring the Mother"? The nurturer
would be
But, you kill, steal, murder her, nurturing
ability. Destroying earth, skies, chil-
dren, and all human lives for RELI-
GIOUSITY!
Oh, Shame, Mockery, Hypocrisy.
Arrogantly insisting all bow down,
To insane demands, continuing to make
killer weapons, the power He thinks He
has in his hands (are weapons of his
destruction)
No more bowing down to male-dominant
irresponsibility',
Or being victims of misogyny.
They have created weapons to destroy all
humanity.

Women, as you stand by, thinking you are
    living,
That you have arrived,
Your men, your sons, your husbands are
    burying you alive. Your sons pick up
    guns and build bombs to drop on other
    sons. Out of control. How do you
    explain this one?
You have the power to show at this hour.
Without the womb man's cooperation,
There is no flow. He and all humans that
    come to the earth come through the
    womb, so to control her life, he makes
    her his wife. Remove the warmongers
    and murderers from your beds, come
    out of their kitchen, let them feed from
    their hands, and stop fixing their
    wounds to kill another man.
No more aiding and abiding by this terri-
    fying man-made plan, Men's terrorist
    police state. Women, if you must?
    Evacuate!
You must assume the position, in your
    hands, is humanity's children's fate.
Stand " Woman of all nations, sisters,
    mothers, daughters of Ma,
It's your womb, your wisdom, your heart,

*That places the power in your hands over
    the wickedness of man.*
Mother of Creation has a healing plan.
*There is no lack of food, just men standing
    in the way, keeping you and your chil-
    dren impoverished with war games they
    play; get them out of your way.*
Don't worry about men taking your lives,
*They have taken them already, made it a
    living hell,*
*Once you take it back, it will be worse for
    them,*
Then, being dead (in prison or jail)
They have not only taken yours,
*They have taken the lives of the ones you
    have born.*
*I made them into cannon fodder for their
    wars.*
Your life is eternal.
*He can't take it, he didn't give it, he would
    only relieve it of the lifelong suffering
    he inflicted.*
*No more murder weapons! Womb-men
    must stand.*
*Her body must come as one be not afraid of
    death.*
THERE is none!

All the womb men on this earth are the
    Mother's Sun!
Light the world with your love,
Shut down this wicked man and his gun!
From this cycle of pain
It must stop now. It's inhuman; it's insane.
He was given the privilege to honor and
    protect,
He chooses to kill, abuse, neglect, and make
    an excuse for this wreck he's made of
    life.
Womb men of the world join hearts, come
    as one.
These weapons men have built.
To kill other humans is an abomination.
They must be dismantled. They must be
    dissolved. They must no longer be
    allowed.
"Wombman of the world, hear this voice,
NEDA, calling out loud! Stand in liberty!
    Stand for love! Stand for life & put
    away the SHROUD.
You can. You must make life worth living.
Who else will the children trust?
You brought them here.
Mother, sister, daughter, brother, we must
    do what we must.

Join hearts and hands with the men who
*   love you, who lift you to your proper*
*   place, healing the whole human race. In*
*   our midst, in our hands, only you.*
*   Mother, sister, daughter, and brother*
*   who love life can free our lives once we*
*   stand. Do it for the children you have*
*   brought; do it for healing, the fulfill-*
*   ment of paradise.*
When you remove the power from this evil
*   man's hands.*
"Neda, Neda, the sound of your name,
"So beautiful, so sweet."
Your voice, so strong, cries out to we
"Women empowerment," the stance
*   must be,*
Here we have the "Victory."

Chapter 4

This is the Response to the Request When Asked for Me to Run for President of the United States Of America, 1992:

"Greetings in the name of the Most High!"

As Jah LOVE goes before I, RASTAFARI, and as Christ's truth is within I, and as ALL L AW, all discipline surrounds me, NONE can come against I.

Give thanks and praise to His Imperial Majesty, Emperor Haile Selassie I, for the words that he spoke to the League of Nations on behalf of peace...

UNTIL THE PHILOSOPHY that holds one race superior and another inferior is finally and permanently discredited and abandoned, then everywhere is war; until there is no longer a first-class and second-class citizen of any nation, there will be war, until the color of human skin is of no more significant then the color of their eyes, everywhere is war, Until the basic human rights are guaranteed to all without regards to race, it's a war, but Until that day the dream of lasting peace world citizenship and the rule of international morality shall remain. Still, a fleeting illusion to be pursued and never attained everywhere is war!!!

I must add that a part hides! "WAR" has become Entertainment!

It states in our constitution that we who have given our consent to institute this form of government to secure our inalienable rights, and if any form of government becomes destructive, it is our duty to alter or abolish it and to CREATE New government.

And where, by and as we have witnessed that this government is MASS Corruption personified LEGISLATIVE Body, Executive body, Judicial body, corporate body, I, at the REQUEST of the citizens of this planet, intend to respond to your request by running for president. For how much blood must be shed until all our and their children are dead in jail, misled, out fighting for freedom with lead for this evil man's plan, and it's our families that are dead. This government drains your cup; you ignore it, and you get Sucked up, and Our children die, cry, and commit suicide.

No one needs to die to come to a solution; this is just an illusion to justify your children being sent to the slaughter. They only wanted to be educated, but they had to be regulated and systematically disposed of, die in the army, in jail or on drugs...WHY! Because you have

FORGOTTEN that you've given them your consent to govern, and I quote... We hold this truth to be self-evident: that all people are created equal and endowed with certain inalienable rights, and among these are life, liberty, and the pursuit of happiness. That to secure these rights, governments are established among humanity, deriving their just powers from the consent of the governed, that whenever any form of government becomes destructive of these ends, it is the right of the people to alter or abolish it and institute NEW Government.

So, who am I? I am Seifuala AdnorhijahKaya. They call me Sahj. I am a person who has spent ten years of my life in a wheelchair. I was falsely diagnosed with muscular dystrophy and condemned to death or, worse, a nonproductive existence. I contend that the responsibility for my degenerated physical state of existence lies with our governments' inflicted and imposed neglect, abuse, and misuse of the powers we've given them. It's the perpetuation and allowance of the contamination of our environment that has caused, after years and generations, the deterioration of the body of the earth and the bodies of humankind. This contamination has also caused the death of my mother when I was six years old and has, in my opinion, denied me the right to bring forth healthy and happy offspring. Therefore, the inalienable rights of my life, liberty and pursuit of happiness, which this form of government instituted for me or you, have NOT BEEN SECURED.

IN FACT, Though I am physically challenged, I do not consider myself DISABLED. Still, I do see that this nation has been made disabled by MISEDUCATION, MISINFORMATION, The LACK of EDUCATION and the presence of IGNORANCE strategically planned and implemented by the government that we FINAN-CIALLY support with our lives and labor. As for the Environment, the ISSUE of hemp is real, pertinent and URGENT. The Ancients have blessed our earth with this plant so that we would have an energy resource that would allow us to have all the technology without pollution and contamination. Its versatility is incredible. The whole plant is used for various areas. Hemp is used for food, paper, clothes, fuel, medicine, plastics, promoting a healthy environment and more. The book The Emperor Wearing No Clothes is the authoritative account and historical record of the cannabis/hemp prohibition and its resourcefulness; as for the healing, After spending ten years in a wheelchair, I had several major surgeries and began walking with leg braces. One went to college, married my wonderful husband and received my degree in education and counseling. While taking a trip to Atlanta to a believer's convention, we were hit by an eighteen-wheeler truck that killed my husband and put me back in the wheelchair. I wrote about the experience in my book

"RELEASED" THROUGH all of this; the cannabis kept me out of debilitating pain, physical and emotional. I first used cannabis as a teen to ease the pain of knots aligning my spinal cord. The odds have seemed insurmountable, but fortunately, I do not understand the concept of giving up.

I am a human being who inhabits this planet along with other beings: Humans, animals, trees, land, air and water. I am one who cares for these. I am a womb man who brings forth the offspring of humans on this planet, So I represent the womb man who wants to protect the being within her or that came forth from her. I represent you. I represent the ethnicity of the:

> "Richness of culture; though we are a variety,
> the spirit of love must be one."

I am physically challenged, a victim of an assault and the abuse of the body of the earth of humankind. I represent you in the fellowship of your suffering, disfigurement, denial of access, degeneration, and physical and emotional torment. I represent you. The farmers and environmentalists—I represent you, for the earth is my body, the water is my blood, and the air is my breath, and all that is broken in the land, earth, water, and air is broken in WE, the reflection of the human bodies of you and me.

For the humans, Womb men, mothers of humanity,

ethnicity, our rainbow of society, the disabled made to be enabled, the farmers and environmentalists, our life sustainers, if you will unite and stand with me, I WILL.

For as JAH LOVE Go before We, For as Christ Truth is within us, For as Allah discipline and obedience surrounds us NONE Can come against us!

Sign your name to help with my campaign if you'd like me to run and break the cycle of pain and run for president in 2016. For a New day where we won't Study WAR No more and instead CREATE PEACE!"

Chapter 5

FYI *Just So You Know!*

This is how the people have become enslaved and how the U.S. committed treason against them (1930).

A few words to define hypothecated:

Through a letter of hypothecation, a borrower pledges collateral to secure debt.

The U.S. citizen (tenant, franchisee) was registered as a beneficiary of the trust via his or her birth certificate.

In 1933, the federal United States "hypothecated" all of the present and future properties, assets, and labor of their "subjects," the 14th Amendment U.S. citizens, to the Federal Reserve. In return, the Federal Reserve System agreed to extend the federal U.S. corporation the credit "money" substitute it

needed. It had to assign collateral and security to creditors for the loan. The U.S. had no assets; they assigned the private property of their economic slaves to the US citizens as collateral against the unpayable federal debt.

The Platform: S.I.N. & Political Strings

Suggested Materials:

- RELEASED by Kaya Gibson (Book)
- "Divine Intervention," sahjKaya Reggae Music CD
- "Thrilled to Life," sahjKaya's spoken word CD.

Sahj kaya@gmail.com

For more information, google:
TREATY OF AMITY AND ECONOMIC RELATIONS

Between The United States and Ethiopia established two High contracting parties, the U-S- Congress and The Federal Democratic Republic of Ethiopia.

The United States went "bankrupt" in 1933 and was

declared so by Pres. Roosevelt by Executive orders 6073, 61.01, 6711 and 6260 on March 9,1933

The Bankruptcy of the United States is an established fact that the U.S. Federal government was dissolved by the Emergency Banking Act, march 9,1933. 48 Stat. 1. Public Law 89-7 19: declared by Pres. Roosevelt, being bankrupt and Insolvent.

Congressman James Traficant addressing the House: "economic slaves." Robert T, Stafford Act: State of Emergency, Disaster Relief and Emergency Assistance Act Criminal Proceedings Ko. l-CP-2011 War Crimes against Peace/humanity.

The charge and conviction of George Bush & Tony Blair.

U.N.l.D.O United Nations Industrial Development Organization

The Tile United States went "bankrupt" in 1933 and was declared So by Pres. Roosevelt by Executive orders 6073, 6102, 6111 and 6260 on inarch 9,1933

Why is Congressman James Traficant, Jr. in jail? He warned us!

The Bankruptcy of the United States. United States Congressional Record, March 17,1993 (note date) Vol. 33, page H-1303

The Speaker is Rep. James Traficant, Jr. (Ohio) addressing the House:

"Mr. Speaker, we are here now in chapter 11...

Members of Congress are official trustees presiding over the greatest reorganization of any Bankrupt entity in world history, the U.S. Government. We are setting forth, hopefully, a blueprint for our future. There are some who say it is a coroner's report that will lead to our demise."

It is an established fact that the United States Federal Government has been dissolved by the Emergency Banking Act, March 9. 1933.48 Stat. 1. Public Law 89-719: declared by President Roosevelt, being bankrupt and insolvent, HJR 192,73rd Congressional session, June 5, 1933 - Joint Resolution to Suspend the Gold Standard and Abrogate the Gold Clause dissolved the Sovereign Authority of the United States and the official capacities of all United States Governmental Offices, Officers, and Departments and is further evidence that the United States Federal Government exists today in name only.

The receivers of the United States Bankruptcy are the International Bankers via the United Nations, the World Bank and the International Monetary Fund. All United States Offices, Officials, and Departments are now operating within a de facto status in name only under Emergency War Powers. With the Constitutional Republican form of Government now dissolved, the receivers of the Bankruptcy have adopted a new form of government for the United States. This new form of government is known as a Democracy, being an established Socialist/Communist order under a new governor for America. This act was instituted and established by transferring and placing the Office of the Secretary of Treasury to that of the Governor of the International Monetary Fund. Public Law 94-564, page 8, Section H.R. 13955 reads in part: "The U.S. Secretary of Treasury receives no compensation for representing the United States?'

Their lust is for power and control. Since the inception of central banking, they have controlled the fates of nations.. .. The Federal Reserve System is a sovereign power structure separate and distinct from the federal United States government.

In fact, the international bankers used a "Canon Law Trust" as their model, adding stock and naming it a "Joint Stock Trust." The U.S. Congress had passed a law making it illegal for any legal "person" to duplicate a "Joint Stock Trust" in 1873. The Federal Reserve Act was legislated post-facto (to 1870), although post-facto laws are strictly forbidden by the Constitution. [1:9:3]

The Federal Reserve System is a sovereign power structure separate and distinct from the federal United States government. The Federal Reserve is a maritime lender and maritime insurance underwriter to the federal United States, operating exclusively under Admiralty/Maritime law. The lender or underwriter bears the risks, and the Maritime law compelling specific performance in paying the interest or premiums are the same.

Assets of the debtor can also be hypothecated (to

pledge something as a security without taking possession of It.) as security by the lender or underwriter. The Federal Reserve Act stipulated that the interest on the debt was to be paid in gold. There was no stipulation in the Federal Reserve Act for ever paying the principal.

Prior to 1913, most Americans owned clear, allodia title to property, free and clear of any liens or mortgages until the Federal Reserve Act (1913) "Hypothecated" all property within the federal United Slates to the Board of Governors of the Federal Reserve, -in which the Trustees (stockholders) held legal title. The U.S. citizen (tenant, franchisee) was registered as a "beneficiary" of the trust via his/her birth certificate. In 1933, the federal United States hypothesized all of the present mid-future properties, assets, and labor of their "subjects," the 14th Amendment U.S. citizen, to the Federal Reserve System.

In return, the Federal Reserve System agreed to extend the federal United States Corporation all the credit "money substitute" it needed. Like any other debtor, the federal United States government had to assign collateral and security to their creditors as a condition of the loan. Since the federal United States didn't have any assets, they assigned the private property of their "economic slaves," the U.S. citizens, as collateral against the unpayable federal debt. They also pledged the unincorporated federal territories, national parks, forests, birth certificates, and nonprofit organizations as collateral against the federal debt. Ail has already been transferred as payment to the international bankers.

The federal United States government and the U.S. Congress were not and have never been authorized by the Constitution for the United States of America to issue currency of any kind, but only lawful money -gold and silver coin.

It is essential that we comprehend the distinction between real money and paper money substitutes. One cannot get rich by accumulating money substitutes; one can only get deeper into debt. We, the People, no longer have any "money." Most Americans have not been paid any [11] money" for a very long time, perhaps not in their entire life. Now, do you comprehend why you feel broke? Now, do you understand why you are "bankrupt," along with the rest of the country?

Federal Reserve Notes (FRNs) are unsigned checks written on a closed account. FRNs are an inflatable paper system designed to create debt through inflation (devaluation of currency). Whenever there is an increase in the supply of a money substitute in the economy without a corresponding increase in the gold and silver backing, inflation occurs.

Inflation is an invisible form of taxation that irresponsible governments inflict on their citizens. The Federal Reserve Bank, which controls the supply and movement of FRNs, has fooled everybody. They have access to an unlimited supply of FRNs, paying only for the printing costs of what they need. FRNs are nothing more than promissory notes for U.S. Treasury securities (T-Bills) - a promise to pay the debt to the Federal Reserve Bank.

There is a fundamental difference between "paying" and "discharging" a debt. To pay a debt, you must pay with value or substance (i.e., gold, silver, barter or a commodity). With FRNs, you can only discharge a debt. You cannot pay a debt with a debt currency system. You cannot service a debt with a currency that has no backing in value or substance. No contract in Common law is valid unless it involves an exchange of "good & valuable consideration." Unpayable debt transfers power and control to the sovereign power structure that has no interest in money, law, equity or justice because they have so much wealth already.

Their lust is for power and control. Since the inception of central banking, they have controlled the fates of nations.

The Federal Reserve System is based on the Canon law and the principles of sovereignty protected in the Constitution and the Bill of Rights.

Gold and silver were such powerful money during the founding of the United States of America that the founding fathers declared that only gold or silver coins could be "money" in America. Since gold and silver coinage were heavy and inconvenient for a lot of transactions, they were stored in banks, and a claim check was issued as a money substitute. People traded their coupons as money, or "currency." Currency is not money but a money substitute. Redeemable currency must promise to pay a dollar equivalent in gold or silver money. Federal Reserve Notes (FRNs) make no such promises and are not "money," A Federal Reserve Note is a debt obligation of the federal United States government, not "money?'

Unwittingly, America has returned to its pre-American Revolution, feudal roots whereby all land is held by a sovereign and the common people had no rights to hold allodia title to property. Once again, we, the People, are the tenants and sharecroppers renting our property from a Sovereign in the guise of the Federal Reserve Bank. We, the people, have exchanged one master for another.

This has been going on for over eighty years without the "informed knowledge" of the American people, without a voice protesting loud enough. Now, it's easy to grasp why America is fundamentally bankrupt. Why don't more people own their properties outright? Why 90% of Americans are mortgaged to the hilt and have little or no assets after all debts and liabilities have been paid? Why does it feel like you are working harder and harder and getting less and less?

We are reaping what has been sown, and the results of our harvest are a painful bankruptcy and a foreclosure on American property, precious liberties, and a way of life.

Few of our elected representatives in Washington, D.C., have dared to tell the truth. The federal United States is bankrupt. Our children will inherit this unpayable debt and the tyranny to enforce paying it. America has become completely bankrupt in world leadership, financial credit and its reputation for courage, vision and human rights. This is an undeclared economic war, bankruptcy, and economic slavery of the most corrupt order! Wake up America! Take back your Country."

Editor's note:

In 2002, Traficant was indicted on federal corruption charges for taking campaign funds for personal use. Again, he opted to represent himself, insisting that the trial was part of a vendetta against him dating to his 1983 trial. On April 15, he was convicted of 10 felony counts, including bribery, racketeering, and tax evasion. In order to get a conviction, the prosecution refused him witnesses, made deals with men who committed more serious crimes for their testimony and, as one witness now admits, goaded false testimony out of their witnesses.

In March 2004, the Federal Bureau of Prisons moved Traficant to the Federal Correctional Institution, Ray Brook. As of July 2007, the Federal Bureau of Prisons listed Traficant at the Federal Medical Center, Rochester, and an administrative facility providing specialized mental health services. Traficant has taken up artwork while in prison. Readers may write to Jim at:

James A. Traficant, Jr. #31213-060, Federal Medical Center PMB 4000, Rochester, MN 55903

A friend commented to me last summer that I didn't own my home: he added that if I had an "Allodia" deed, I might be better off. After searching the web, which contains a lot of information on allodia deeds, etc., 1 discovered this article in the March 17,2008 issue of The Free Press, located at PO Box 293339, Kerrville, TX 78029.

The Bankruptcy of the United States

Mar 17,1993 ... It is an established fact that the United States Federal Government has been dissolved.... In return, the Federal Reserve System agreed to extend the federal United States Corporation all the credit "money substitute" it needed

The Bankruptcy of the United States

United States Congressional Record, March 17,1993 Vol. 33, page H-1303

Untitled Document

1815 president

James Madison proposed a second privately owned owned Bank of the United States which was chartered in 1816 and opened in 1817.

In 1836 overriding Congress, Jackson closed the Bank of the United States commenting:

"The bold effort the present bank had made to control the government are but premonitions of the fate that await the

American people should they be deluded into a perpetuation of this institution or the establishment of another like it."

In 1846 The Independent Treasury Act is approved.

Following Lincoln's threat of invasion if States refused to pay the 52% Morrill tax, ten southern States lawfully secede from the Union between December 1860 and February 1851:

"The power confided to me will be used to hold, occupy, and possess the property and places belonging to the Government and to collect the duties and Imposts; but beyond what may be necessary for these objects, there will be no Invasion, no using of force against or among the people anywhere." Abraham Lincoln in his Inaugural Address Monday, March 4, 1861

Against the advice of his generals and congress, Lincoln initiated the so-called "Civil War" In April of 1861, one month after Abraham Lincoln was inaugurated. In his inaugural speech Lincoln promised to do nothing about slavery: "I have no purpose, directly or indirectly, to Interfere with the institution of slavery in the

States where It exists. I believe I have no lawful right to do so, and I have no inclination to do so." It was only when Lincoln was losing the war that he issued the emancipation proclamation where he proclaimed that slaves in the Nations of the Confederate States were free.

To pay for the 'civil war, on the 5th of August 1861, Congress passes the first National Income tax and by the 21st of that month the first paper currency was issued.

Lincoln said, "The money powers prey upon the nation in times of peace and conspire against it in times of adversity. The banking powers are more despotic than a monarchy, more insolent than autocracy, more selfish than bureaucracy. They denounce as public enemies all who question their methods are throw light upon their crimes. I have two great enemies, the Southern Army in front of me and the bankers in the rear. Of the two, the one at my rear is my greatest foe. Corporations have been enthroned, and an era of corruption in high places will follow. The money power of the country will endeavor to prolong its reign.by working upon the prejudices of the people until the wealth is aggregated in the hands of a few, and the Republic is destroyed."

In February 1863, Congress established another National Banking system. The bankers were intending to charge between 24% and 36% interest rates for money to finance the war. To avoid the Interest, Lincoln ordered the printing of $450 million in bank notes guaranteed by the U.S. government.

MY DUTY

We have CERTAIN INALIENABLE Rights, which are inalienable, given by the creator, 30 human rights in fact. Human riqhts.com states that if ANY form of government becomes DESTRUCTIVE, these rights are not secured or protected. As the constitution states, it is our right and, in fact, our DUTY to alter or ABOLISH it And Create a New government that provides for the humans that they are put in place to serve in the securing and protection of all humans and cultures. The design and strategy of the governments not only of the United States but of the world. As we move in and try to adjust to the twenty-first century, we have done worse than words can describe; our whole existence displays it in all the blood that has been shed and continues to increase in the shedding of blood. Slaughter. Some seem to think that continuing to do things the same way and that somehow there will be different results; we all know and would agree that this is NOT true, and we consider it insane thinking. Correct... However. Although the humans had given their CONSENT to be governed, the constitution gives them the right to create a new government. Yes. But not by storming buildings, killing, stealing, and destroying with man-made fatal tinker toys called guns and poison gas. But in the transition of governance that is represented by humane beings in a variety of beautiful, unique cultures.

It is uniting for EQUAL HUMAN RIGHTS Globally. This is A New World that we all can Live with, literally. This change comes by educating humans what their human rights are (humanrights.com) and joining, The Humane Race Party, unifiedexchange.org. It is Equalitarian. Equal. Period. It is not Democrat; it is not Republican; it is not black; it is not white; it's not gay; it's not straight. It's not male; it's not female. It's THE HUMAN(ane) RACE PARTY. It is a new day, a new time; it is time for new ways of governance of human beings in humanity. We have allowed man-made concepts, religions, miseducation, and misinformation to literally create confusion and conflict throughout the world. Placing all in the clutches of mental, emotional, and religious deceitful enslavement, there is a better plan for our new world: no longer feeding into the competition sickness and the human identity crisis.

Join today. Unifiedexchange.org
The Truth about the Human Identity Crisis

Chapter 6

Assault On Humans

Accused u, they murder your poor.Do the police protect, or do they make you sweat, feel threat, intimidated and distressed? So why is it they murdered you, and you are still paying? They check, abuse, murder, disrespect, and believe half of what you see and none of what you hear! Media, you watching you on the news on the tube, it seems all you have is doom, not true, not true, only if you choose to continue to do& allow the evil done thru you...

LOVE SHALL MOVE MOUNTAINS, AND THE TRUTH IS THE SOURCE THAT WILL

REMOVE WAR & DEATH FROM OUR DOOR & I+S+US CHRIST ONE COME & I+S+US WILL BE DONE IN EARTH BY THE SPIRIT OF CHRIST IN OUR MINDS NOT CONFUSING DOCTRINES THAT DIVIDE, IT IS THE BODY OF I+S+US THE HANDS THAT BRINGS JUST US I+S+US WE BREAK THE CYCLE OF PAIN, ALLOW LIGHT IN YOUR LIFE, THEN YOU WILL SEE TRUTH LIGHT EXPOSUREMAKES YOU FREE, VICTIMS OF WAR, WANT TO HEAR SOME MORE TRUTH IS A VICTIM OF WAR, IS ANYBODY KEEPING SCORE COUNTING THE LIES OF THE BEAST, THE WHORE PRINCIPLES OF DARKNESS COVERING BLATANT LIES SHOOTING MISSILES OF DESTRUCTION HUMANITY's CHILDREN DIES, TRUTH IS A VICTIM MOCKED WITH BOMB LIT SKYS, IF YOU LISTEN YOU WILL HEAR LOVE CRIES WHEN YOU DO IT TO THE LEAST OF THESE U DO IT UNTO ME, ALL BECAUSE THE LUST THE EGO THE VANITY THE TOTAL DISREGARD FOR THE TREE FROM WHICH U BREATHE WAR IS THE ENEMY U HOLD TRUTH A VICTIM WHEN IT CAN ONLY SET U FREE.

HOW MUCH BLOOD MUST BE SHED TIL ALL HUMANS ARE TORMENTEDBDEAD IN JAIL, MISLED, FIGHT FREEDOM WITH LEAD?

IT ITS MORE SOMEBODY'S CHILDREN DEAD, CONGRESS; HOW MANY OF YOURS DID YOU OFFER UO? THE GOVERNMENT DRAINS YOUR CUP YOU IGNORE IT AND GET SUCKED UP CHILDREN CRY MORE DIE. CAN YOU HEAR THEM WAITING TO COME HOME? LISTEN, CAN YOU HEAR OR DO U CARE? No one needs to die TO COME TO A SOLUTION. THIS IS JUST AN ILLUSION TO JUSTIY YOUR SUNS SENT TO A SLAUGHTER TO DIE. THEY ONLY WANTED TO BE EDUCATED, BUT REALLY THEY'VE been regulated SYSTEMATI-CALLY DISPOSED OF DIE IN THE ARMED FORCES, JAIL OR ON DRUGS WHY WHY WHY U FORGOT YOU'd GIVEN THEM CONTROL OF YOUR LIFE, Bloodied Battlefield mingled with oil, How dare you let them go to die for a mock, you know mockery to a men command a wombless man I Womb Man. How can you bring it forth, then take away its life to live, giving it up to a burning bush, or abomination the death angels to humans, the death angel of the earth seas skies cry the death angel to humanity the father of lies Shooting in the skies the death angel a voice in the burning lying bush speaks with fork tongue death and destruc-tion hypocrites, and the fool has said in his heart there is no god but me, Manmade concept of god and religions: Purpose: to control and dominate the human beings.

I was born to find the answers to the cure for humanity. Why the pain and suffering? From the start, Misinformation miseducation, campaign, animal husbandry-weaponized education, and the doctrine of discovery. General Education Board member Frederick T. Gates: "In our dream, we have limitless resources, and the people yield themselves with perfect docility to our molding hand. We shall not search for embryo great artists, painters, musicians, lawyers, doctors, preachers, politicians, or statesmen, of whom we have an ample supply; the task we set before ourselves is very simple as well as a very beautiful one, to train these people as we find them to a perfectly ideal life just where they are."

The deception began at the beginning: his story as a man separated himself from humans to rule over and dominate humans by controlling their minds through miseducation, deceit, and brainwashing.

He was sent to reveal the source of deception and its impact on the war on humankind Through the only effective weapon that man devised in his ego mind.

> "And god saw that the wickedness of man was
> great in the earth and that every imagination
> of the thoughts of his heart was only evil
> continually and it repented the lord that he

had made man on the earth and it grieved
him at his heart, numbers 23:19 god is not a
man, that he should lie;"

— genesis 5, 6

Even a man who had separated himself from humans
began his great deception and began to use the weapon
that would deplete the power of the human by dividing it
against itself. This weapon is to divide and conquer.

Humans were created as humans; one human was
created with a(as you call it) womb, and the other human
was created without a womb. The womb was created as a
place to reproduce or manufacture a human biological
"suit" that was compatible with the environment that it
would need to function and thrive in; it created the host
for the energy spirit being would use to enjoy and explore
what the divine intelligent, eternal energy of what is called
life.

So the wombless human being threatened by the
human with a womb and their ability to reproduce more
humans determined it was necessary to create division by
making himself a god and giving himself power over the
human with a womb and to control it and all that it reproduced. By giving it labels, titles, categories, and a hierarchy
of which the god he created himself had all authority, he
created religions to support his diabolical plan.

Most people, to this day, because of this deception, conditioning, and manipulation, have no idea who they are. They are unable to find their true selves because the foundation of knowledge they have is based on lies. They are spiritually diseased or ill at ease because of the confusion they experience due to not knowing the energy balance of feminine/masculine. Defining humans as gender establishes a competition of values, strengths and weaknesses by gender as part and beginning of the tool of divisiveness to diminished authority or power of one being. Everyone wants to know who they are but can't correctly access who they are or have incorrect information to determine what the answer would be. Human beings ARE GOOD/LOVE eternal energy being inside anatomical biological "human beings in a variety of unique and beautiful cultures. Being indoctrinated as a man or woman has created a spiritual disease, imbalance and Identity crisis. When you come to know your true self and all the choices that have been taken from you through deceit, then humans can be healed of this spiritual disease and resolve the identity crisis. That causes them to filter all their life sources and energy through a glass darkly based on gender and other modalities. Instead of knowing and recognizing that all the things that make a human are not gender, such as love, integrity, honesty, generosity, discipline, creativity, morality etc..etc..etc...The energy-intelligent, omnipotent energy from whence we were manifested, such as Love/Good, is neither created, destroyed, ageless, timeless and is all good except that which man pk from good to create an idol/idle god of lust to feed his ego of power and domination throughout the world having humans divided against themselves in ignorance to the will of his deception. There is GOOD energy, NO go; there is no good energy, no deil, only the energy that vibrates in the human who realizes the energy and determines by choice to use it for good/love for self and others or evil for themselves and against others...

To know their true selves and not "believe" the lies told to them about themselves. Understand the balance of who they are and the choices they have for their lives.

Life begins when the energy of life enters the reproduced suit, and the breath carries the spirit in.

Know that there is no god or devil; these are artificial concepts to hold you captive.

There is no such thing as death; this is a man-made concept.

That you were originally sent/came here for enjoyment.

That you have the right to choose to live here as well as the choice not to, without condemnation.

Chapter 7

A vision for the Future of humankind

7 Point Plan to End Poverty in the United States

As the wealthiest country in the world, with high productivity per capita and a country that produces an abundance of capital, credit, technology, and food, we can end poverty. Yet, according to the Bureau of the Census, poverty and hunger for children and adults are increasing rather than decreasing - 34.6 million Americans live in deep poverty, 12.1% of the U.S. population. Many millions of Americans live in what is called "near poverty" by the Labor Department. We must make ending poverty a priority and weave that goal into a network of policies:

- Truly Progressive Taxation
- An End to Huge Corporate Subsidies and Military Budget Waste

- Job Creation
- Equal Pay for Women
- Child-Care
- Living Wages for All Workers
- Restore the critical Social Safety Net.

Expand Worker's Rights by Developing an Employee Bill of Rights

The rights of workers have been on the decline. It is time to reverse that trend and begin to give workers the backbone of the US economy the rights they deserve. Workers need a living wage, not a minimum wage, access to health care and no unilateral reductions in medical benefits and pensions for current employees and retirees. Employers should not be able to avoid these benefits by hiring "temporary workers" or "independent contractors."

The privacy of employees needs to be vigorously protected. The notorious Taft-Hartley Act, which makes it extremely difficult for employees to organize unions, needs to be repealed. It has resulted in less than 10% of the private workforce being unionized, the lowest in 60 years and the lowest percentage in the Western world. Non-union workers need upgraded rights against Walmart.

Toward Consumer Justice

The enforcement of consumer protection laws, especially against the terrible abuses in low-income communities, needs to be given the leadership and resources required. Neither party in control of our city nor the national government has been concerned with such predatory practices.

The poor pay more and are expendable to them. Hundreds of billions of dollars annually are taken from consumers due to computerized billing fraud, unconscionable credit and financial services charges, price gouging, shoddy merchandise, phony repairs, bogus medical treatments, medical malpractice, real estate scams, identity thefts, and other fraudulent regularly reported and neglected crimes.

There needs to be more, not less, civil action rights to pursue in court, both economic and legal.

http://citizensforgibson.com/issues.htm 8/10/2004

Grievances and wrongful injuries under a preserved and expanded tort system that internalizes the costs of misconduct and enlarges deterrence. Safety standards from motor vehicles to pharmaceuticals and household products need serious enhancement to save lives and injuries and prevent diseases.

Fair Tax Where the Wealthiest and Corporations Pay their Share

The complexity and distortions of the tax code produce distributions of lax incidence and payroll tax burdens that are skewed in favor of the wealthy and the corporations further garnished by tax shelters, insufficient enforcement and other avoidances.

Corporate tax contributions as a percent of the overall federal revenue stream have been declining for fifty years and now stand at 7.4X despite massive record profits. A fundamental reappraisal of «jr tax laws should start with a principle that taxes should apply first to behavior and conditions we 3 favor least and pinch necessities least, such as the clearly addictive industries (alcohol and tobacco), pollution, speculation, gambling, extreme luxuries, taxing work or instead of the 5% to 7%sales tax food, furniture, clothing or books.

Tiny taxes (a fraction of the conventional retail sales percentage) on stock, bond, and derivative transactions can produce tens of billions of dollars a year and displace some of the taxes on work and consumer essentials.

Reproductive Health

Waiting periods, informed consent requirements, bans on public funding, insurance prohibitions, unnecessary clinic regulations - these laws are not designed to protect women. Instead, they are designed to deter women from choosing abortion and to make it more difficult and burdensome to obtain for those who do.

Part Two

In the FACE of tyranny: Unite for Community Uprising. Commemorating the anniversary of the million women march that International Wombmen's Day!

BEBOLDFORCHANGE!

A New Plan, Corporate overhaul.

HUMAN REVOLUTION!

Priestess/Minister MAtemple Sanctuary of Life, Author, Artist, Activist

Location: (TBC)

MOTHER'S DAY CELEBRATION!

RISE OF THE WOMBMAN!

Who is SHE? Who are YOU?

Building for the Wombman Sabbath Celebration

1. Serenade Prepare to Be Pampered Reception
2. Song Poetry Humor Issues A Conversation
3. .MASS INCARCERATION.21 CENTURY SLAVERY Human Abomination, What to do.
4. .Wars & Rumors of War and How to Shut it Down.
5. .Marriage Union: The Truth & The Lie
6. .Chant Down Babylon PAHELLENIC Step Show
7. .White Supremacy Institutions?! Yeah, I said it! Comedy, or is it?
8. .MASS DETRUCTIVE WEAPONS?! GUNS & BOMBS!

Stop the Clock. Reset humanity.

The plan for the Wombman of the World, The Anointed, The Chosen for the Salvation of Humanity!

1. Economic Ethical Powerbase. A nation prepared!
2. S.I.N, Self-Inflicted Nonsense RELIGION. POLITICS.INALIENABLE? Right?
3. The Abomination: Whose Children Are These? Child ABUSE Abandoned

1. Mother's Recognitions

BLUE BAND: Mothers whose child has been murdered or maimed by police, RED BAND: Mothers whose child was murdered or maimed in the war around the world, for all blood is red.

YELLOW BAND: Mother, child murdered or maimed by Chemical warfare, disease, vaccines, medical malpractice

BLACK BAND: Missing loved ones.

V.I.P. GUEST TBA

"A Call for Sororities & Fraternities" Human rights education

unifiedexchange.orgsahjkaya@gmail.com
816-616-8497

TO: THE DIVINE 9

AS THE DIVINE NINE, WE HAVE BECOME PART OF A BODY, EVEN A ZION TRAIN OF OPPORTUNITY, FOR THE ROAD TO TRUE FREEDOM AND HAPPINESS FOR THE HUMANITY WE REPRESENT. WE ARE A PART OF A BODY WHOSE MISSION IS

TO SERVE, UPLIFT AND EMPOWER THEM, WE, US, THROUGH EDUCATION. THE BASIC AND MOST FUNDAMENTAL EDUCATION, NOT TO MENTION ESSENTIAL, IS THAT ONE MUST KNOW THEIR HUMAN RIGHTS SO THAT THEY CAN UPHOLD THEM FOR THEIR PROTECTION, DEFENSE, AND SAFETY.

HEREIN LAYS OUR OPPORTUNITY TO SERVE IN A MASSIVE WAY, IN THE GREATEST CAPACITY, WITH THE MOST IMPORTANT TOOL FOR HUMANITY IN OUR TIME. THERE IS NO MORE IMPORTANT TIME THAN NOW, NEITHER A MORE IMPORTANT SUBJECT NOR PROJECT, BECAUSE IN THIS TIME, EVERY MOVE IS BEING MADE TO TAKE AWAY ALL HUMAN RIGHTS FROM THE PEOPLE. PEOPLE ARE NOT AWARE BECAUSE THEY LACK KNOWLEDGE OF THESE 30 UNIVERSAL HUMAN RIGHTS. HUMANS BECOME SLAVES AND SUBJECTS AND VICTIMS OF ABUSE BY WAY OF A LACK OF KNOWLEDGE OF THESE RIGHTS, WHICH ARE AVAILABLE FOR THEM TO HAVE.

THUS, WHAT IS MOST IMPORTANT IN THIS SHIFT OUR WORLD IS TAKING IS

ALL ABOUT SERVICE AND EDUCATION.

THIS INSPIRED ME TO CONTACT YOU. TO MAKE YOU AWARE OF THIS CAMPAIGN AND THE IMPACT WE, THE DIVINE 9, WOULD

MAKE EDUCATING AND SERVING OUR COMMUNITIES WITH THIS INFORMA-TION. IT IS THE UNITED FOR HUMAN RIGHTS CAMPAIGN THAT IS ALREADY CHANGING OUR WORLD.

INCLUDED WITH THIS LETTER IS A PACKAGE SHOWING THE IMPACT IT HAS MADE. OUR ASSISTANCE WOULD BE MONUMENTAL AND UNIFYING! I CAN'T IMAGINE A GREATER SERVICE OR EDUCATION WE CAN OFFER.

PLEASE REVIEW THE CONTENTS AND DISCUSS IT. LET US AGREE TO UNITE, TO FREE HUMAN BEINGS FROM A LACK OF KNOWLEDGE OF THEIR RIGHTS AS A HUMAN BEING.

IN RECOGNIZING THE IMPORTANCE OF THE KNOWLEDGE OF ONE'S HUMAN RIGHTS, WE ALSO RECOGNIZE THERE IS THE NEED FOR A FORA PARTY THAT UPHOLDS THESE RIGHTS, THUS ARRISE THE HUMAN RACE PARTY, RUN BY HUMAN BEINGS, NOT THOSE WITH ANIMALISTIC

TENDENCIES REPRESENTED BY DONKEYS,
ELEPHANTS, OR ANY OTHER ANIMAL BUT
HUMANS WHO ARE THE CARETAKERS
OF ALL.
    THANK YOU FAMILY,
AMBASSADOR SAHJ KAYA

sahjkaya@gmail.com

HUMANRIGHTS.ORG
DELTA SIGMA THETA EPSILON PSI
UNITED TRADE COUNCIL
HUMAN RACE PARTY
UNIFIEDEXCHANGE.ORG
UnitedTradeCouncil (unifiedexchange.org)
DIVINE 9

- **Alpha Phi Alpha Fraternity**
- **Alpha Kappa Alpha Sorority**
- **Kappa Alpha Psi Fraternity**
- **Omega Psi Phi Fraternity**
- **Delta Sigma Theta Sorority**
- **Phi Beta Sigma Fraternity**
- **Zeta Phi Beta Sorority**
- **Sigma Gamma Rho Sorority**
- **Lota Phi Theta Fraternity**

INSTITUTIONS for the healing of humanity through Source Inspiration

- MAAT TEMPLE
- CAMPUS
- CAREER, EMPLOYMENT,
- ENTREPRENEURSHIP TRAINING INSTITUTE
- IRAQ
- HTH. - Hiring The Heritage, C.E.E.T. Institute Inc.
- MAAT Temple Sanctuary of Life Wellness Center
- MAAT Stars Family Entertainment Arena, featuring: 7 Culture Dinner Theater, state-of-the-art HolyRoller, Roller Skating Rink, Electronic Robotic Game Room, Vestro delicatessen, Children Feature Movie Theater

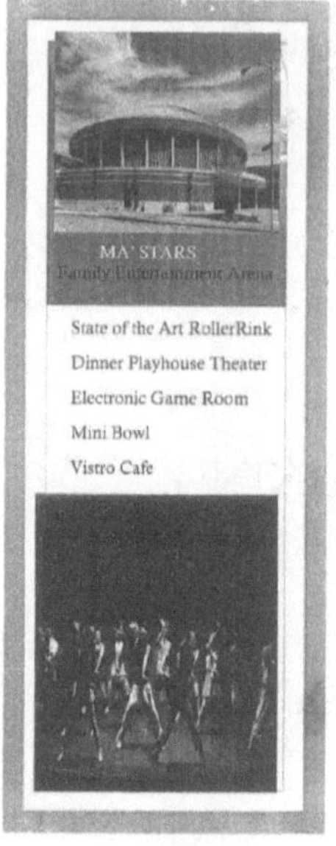

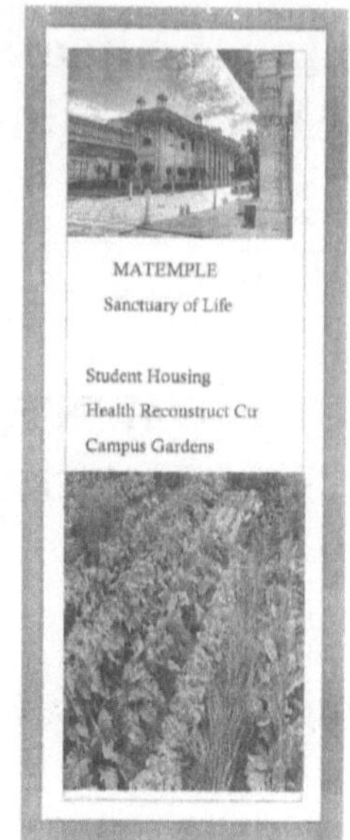

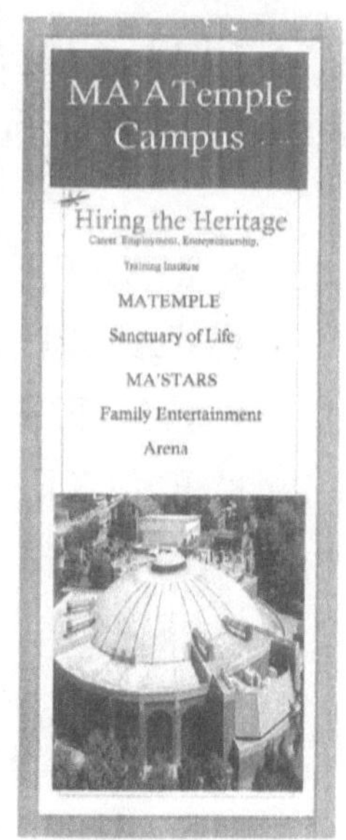

MONEY MANAGEMENT ORGANIZATION
COMMUNITY AWARENESS/ ACTIVITY
TAXATION COMPREHENSION SELF-DEFENSE
TEACHING TRAINING INTERNSHIP
CULINARY ARTS DEGREE
CATERING TO ALL CULTURES MFEA, KUUMBA
DinnerPlayhouse
CRAFT OUR CULTURES MFEAKUUMBADinner
Playhouse
CREATIVE PRODUCTIONS MFEAKUUMBADin-
nerPlayhouse
Business Accounting, Bookkeeping, inventory MFEAKU-
UMBADinnerPlayhouse

CLEAN UP CREWS MA'AT TEMPLE CAMPUS
I-REFLECTION PRESS ON
NEIGHBORHOOD ELDERLY BRUNCH CLUB
& CHILDCARE
MA TEMPLE SANCTUARY OF LIFE

Mission

To improve the quality of life for economically and educationally disadvantaged persons through educational, cultural, human and spiritual development training.

How to live as a human being
Spiritual health
Mental health
Physical health
MA STARS FAMILY ENTERTAINMENT ARENA
KUUMBA DINNER PLAYHOUSE
STATE OF THE ART ROLLER RINK
DJ BOOTH
ELECTRONIC GAME ROOM
VISTRO FUD BAR
ANNUAL FUNDRAISING EVENTS
Salute to the Heritage of Humanity "Tribute Series
Summer Serenade
Seven days of Kwanzaa "Culturally Yours"
Reignbow for Peace Humanitarian Gathering

Thriller Night Costume Ball
Torch of Dreams Awards Benefit Cultural Festival Dinner
National Tap Dance Day Skating Competitions Game
tournaments
MAAT TEMPLE
CAMPUS
CAREER, EMPLOYMENT,
ENTREPRENEURSHIP TRAINING INSTITUTE
ZIMBABWE
HTH. - Hiring The Heritage, C.E.E.T. Institute Inc.
MAAT Temple Sanctuary of Life Wellness Center
MAAT Stars Family Entertainment Arena, featuring: 7
Culture Dinner Theater, state-of-the-art HolyRoller,
Roller Skating Rink, Electronic Robotic Game Room,
Vetsro delicatessen, Children Feature Movie Theater
CAMPUS
C.E.E.T.I.
MATemple Sanctuary

MA'Stars Entertainment Arena

C.E.E.T.I

Career, Employment, Entrepreneurship, Training
Institute

MAAT TEMPLE

CAREER, EMPLOYMENT,
ENTREPRENEURSHIP TRAINING INSTITUTE
VIET NAM

STATE OF MISSOURI

John R. Ashcroft
Secretary of State

CERTIFICATE OF RESCISSION

I, JOHN R. ASHCROFT, Secretary of State of the State of Missouri, hereby certify that the forfeiture/administrative dissolution entered against

REGINALD GIBSON MEMORIAL FOUNDATION
N00044170

on 12/21/2010, as provided in the State of Missouri Nonprofit Corporation Act was this day rescinded, and said corporation was on this date hereby restored to good standing in the records of this office.

IN TESTIMONY WHEREOF, I hereunto set my hand and cause to be affixed the GREAT SEAL of the State of Missouri. Done at the City of Jefferson, this 15th day of October, 2018.

Secretary of State

The Reginald J. Gibson Memorial Foundation was established to memorialize a man who should not be forgotten, a man who loved God for the love and truth he found in God and shared that love and integrity with all who came in contact with him. He knew truth and lived it, spoke it, and shared it with all, even those who resisted it, for he knew that the spirit of truth is the integrity of God. As he knew the truth, he also knew the salvation of education and the devastation of those who had fallen victim to miseducation and misinformation, leaving the victims unstable and unable to make their lives better. Therefore, the Foundation was designed specifically to assist the educationally and economically disadvantaged in improving their quality of life. The Reginald J. Gibson Foundation, rebranded as the United Trade Council, is located in Kansas City, Missouri.

The primary mission of the Gibson Foundation is to fund and support "Hiring the Heritage[1]- a career employment entrepreneurship training program that taps into the innate abilities or talents and teaches individuals how to make these talents marketable. This program also offers prerequisite workshops that assist in teaching behavioral disciplines that add to the maintenance and success of these newfound options. Major support (financially and educationally) for 'Hiring the Heritage' are fundraising events sponsored by the foundation that also offer educational stimulation, cultural information and community participation while being pleasantly entertaining and raising fun and funds.

"Hiring the Heritage" is the name of this program and is directly related to the heritage of humanity, those persons who adhere to our motto: "Stepping toward employing people and serving ourselves."

Always remember to help ourselves and help others, for when we help others, we help ourselves.

The Foundation is truly one that exemplifies the hope and the humanity that my husband, Reginald J. Gibson, lived in word and deed. As he lives through me and through this foundation, a seed of life is planted that he may live eternally within all those who benefit from this effort to educate, enlighten and empower.

Robin Carnahan
Secretary of State

CERTIFICATE OF INCORPORATION
MISSOURI NONPROFIT

WHEREAS, Articles of Incorporation of

Hiring the Heritage, Career, Employment, Entrepreneurship, Training Institute, Incorporated
N01230894

have been received and filed in the Office of the Secretary of State, which Articles, in all respects, comply
with the requirements of Missouri Nonprofit Corporation Law;

NOW, THEREFORE, I, ROBIN CARNAHAN, Secretary of the State of Missouri do by virtue of the
authority vested in me by law, do hereby certify and declare this entity a body corporate, duly organized
this date and that it is entitled to all rights and privileges granted corporations organized under the
Missouri Nonprofit Corporation Law.

IN TESTIMONY WHEREOF, I hereunto
set my hand and cause to be affixed the
GREAT SEAL of the State of Missouri.
Done at the City of Jefferson, this
24th day of May, 2012.

Secretary of State

XXS #30 (01-2008)

State of Missouri

Robin Carnahan
Secretary of State

CERTIFICATE OF ORGANIZATION

WHEREAS,

DOMASTARS Family Entertainment Arena LLC
LC1227950

filed its Articles of Organization with this office on the May 16, 2012, and that filing was found to conform to the Missouri Limited Liability Company Act.

NOW, THEREFORE, I, ROBIN CARNAHAN, Secretary of State of the State of Missouri, do by virtue of the authority vested in me by law, do certify and declare that on the May 16, 2012, the above entity is a Limited Liability Company, organized in this state and entitled to any rights granted to Limited Liability Companies.

IN TESTIMONY WHEREOF, I hereunto set my hand and cause to be affixed the GREAT SEAL of the State of Missouri. Done at the City of Jefferson, this May 16, 2012.

Secretary of State

STATE OF MISSOURI

Robin Carnahan
Secretary of State

CERTIFICATE OF TERMINATION

WHEREAS, Articles of Termination of

CannaCaucasA&E LLC
LC0880339

a Limited Liability Company, have been received, found to conform to law, and filed.

NOW, THEREFORE, I, ROBIN CARNAHAN, Secretary of State of the State of Missouri, issue this Certificate of Termination of the aforenamed Limited Liability Company, certifying that the existence of said Limited Liability Company has this date ceased.

IN TESTIMONY WHEREOF, I hereunto set my hand and cause to be affixed the GREAT SEAL of the State of Missouri. Done at the City of Jefferson, this 26th day of May, 2009.

Secretary of State

Robin Carnahan
Secretary of State

CERTIFICATE OF INCORPORATION
MISSOURI NONPROFIT

WHEREAS, Articles of Incorporation of

MATEMPLE Sanctuary of Life Inc.
N01219781

have been received and filed in the Office of the Secretary of State, which Articles, in all respects, comply with the requirements of Missouri Nonprofit Corporation Law;

NOW, THEREFORE, I, ROBIN CARNAHAN, Secretary of the State of Missouri do by virtue of the authority vested in me by law, do hereby certify and declare this entity a body corporate, duly organized this date and that it is entitled to all rights and privileges granted corporations organized under the Missouri Nonprofit Corporation Law.

IN TESTIMONY WHEREOF, I hereunto set my hand and cause to be affixed the GREAT SEAL of the State of Missouri. Done at the City of Jefferson, this 11th day of April, 2012.

Secretary of State

SOS #30 (01-2005)

ALTHOUGH I'M BOMBARDED WITH ALL THE CORRUPTION SPEWING THROUGH THE AIRWAVES,

WITH ALL THE STORIES THAT LEAD PEOPLE IN ALL DIRECTIONS AND AWAY FROM INTEGRITY AND HUMANITY FOCUS COMMUNITY. I'M SEEKING PERSONS WHO COULD COMPREHEND THE STRATEGY FOR RAISING COMMUNITY AND CORRECTING THE NARRATIVE OF THIS "BAD MOVIE" WITH THESE "BAD CHARACTERS' THERE'S TRUTH TO BE TOLD; I AM SENT TO TELL IT, TO LIBERATE AND

EMANCIPATE HUMANITY FROM MENTAL ENSLAVEMENT AND THIS IS ONE WAY IT WILL BE TOLD AND DONE.

I WAS INSPIRED TO CREATE THIS MUSIC, DIVINE INTERVENTION AND THRILLED TO LIFE, AS WELL AS ESTABLISH E.H.R.P. EQUALITARIAN HUMAN RACE PARTY LLC. IT IS WRITTEN, PARAPHRASED, "BY THE PEOPLE'S CONSENT THEY GOVERN WHEN CORRUPTION ABIDES, IT IS TIME TO ALTER OR ABOLISH IT. I AM SENT TO BRING THIS ALTERNATIVE TO THE TABLE. NOT A NEW NARRATIVE BUT THE TRUE NARRATIVE.

ONE REQUEST I HAVE OF YOU, THAT HAVE READ MY EXPERIENCES AND MISSION FOR OUR NEW WORLD, IS TO LISTEN TO MY MUSIC WHICH IS ON YOUTUBE, SPOTIFY, ITUNES. I WOULD APPRECIATE ALL THOSE WHO HAVE EYES< EARS, AND HEARTS THAT WOULD JOIN ME FOR THE RENEWING OF LIFE ON OUR PLANET.

MY MISSION TAKING THE BATON FROM THE HAND OF SO MANY LIKE TUPAC, MALCOLM, MARTIN, HARRIET, SHIRLEY Chisholm, AND SO MANY MORE THAT KEEP ME UP NIGHTS, SO TO SPEAK AND FINISH OUT

THE RACE TO SET THE "CAPTIVES"[1] FREE. I WILL BE ATTEMPTING TO GET THIS TO WHOEVER WILL LISTEN AND HEAR AND HELP. I'VE REBRANDED THE REGINALD GIBSON MEMORIAL FOUNDATION INC 501C3 AS THE UNITED TRADE COUNCIL; MY OTHER COMPANIES HIRING THE HERITAGE A CAREER EMPLOYMENT ENTREPRENEURSHIP TRAINING INSTITUTE INC. MAATTEMPLE SANCTUARY OF LIFE INC(WELLNESS). EXONERATE MA PEOPLE JUSTICE INITIATIVE INC FOR WRONGLY CONVICTED, MASTERS FAMILY ENTERTAINMENT INC. ARENA, TUJA PRODUCTION & PUBLISHING, CANNABIS CAUCUS AGRICULTURE, ENVIRONMENT & EDUCATION, I'M BREAKING THE CEILING ON DREAMING AND MANIFESTING BIG, THESE COMBINED IS MAAT TEMPLE CAMPUS. DESIGNED BY THE SOURCE THAT SENT ME. I'VE WRITTEN A PORTION OF MY STORY IN MY BOOK "RELEASED" BY KAYA GIBSON, AVAILABLE ON AMAZON.COM. I MAY BE CONTACTED AT SAHJKAYA@GMAIL.COM, 816-616-8497., to book speaking engagements.

RADICAL EXTREME ELIMINATE THE THREAT CAMPAIGN, SAHJKAYA FOR PRESI-

DENT, THE PLATFORM: S.I.N. (SELF INFLICTED NONSENSE) & POLITICAL STRINGS(GANGSTER RINGS WORLDWIDE/GLOBAL COLLEGE CAMPUS CAMPAIGN.

"SAHJKAYA WANTS YOU! HUMAN BEINGS!"

— Our Earth's cleanup crew.

HUMANE ENERGY IS IN HUMAN FORM IN A VARIETY OF UNIQUE & BEAUTIFUL CULTURES. EQUAL PERIOD. ELIMINATE THE THREAT!

RESOLVING THE HUMAN IDENTITY CRISIS & HUMAN SPIRITUAL DISEASE, THANK YOU FOR YOUR TIME AND CONSIDERATION. I AM ANOINTED HIGH PRIESTESS SEIFUALA ADNORIJAH KAYA. MAAT TEMPLE SANCTUARY OF LIFE INC.

ALSO KNOWN AS SAHJKAYA, BORN: Rhonda m Gibson: all rights reserved. Flint Michigan

EQUAL PERIOD RADICAL, EXTREME, EQUALITARIAN HUMAN RACE PARTY.LLC, ELIMINATE THE THREAT! SAHJKAYA FOR PRES-IDENT DIVINE INTERVENTION Cd Spoken Word Reggae Music)

THRILLED TO LIFE (Hiphop African Percussion Spoken Word)

Compilation fundraiser for the campaign

DIVINE INTERVENTION:

THRILLED TO LIFE:

CYCLES OF PAIN, KANSAS CITY SHINING BRIGHT, MEDIA A PART HIDES, TIME OUT FOR THE HATERS, LAST DAYS, TOOKIE.

TOWER OF BIBLE, MEDIA A PART HIDES (SPW)/PERCUSSION.

LOVE LOVE LOVE, MY YOKE IS EASY.

REGGAE PARTY, IDOL WORSHIPPERS;

NUCLEAR WEAPONS, DO YOU REALLY LOVE ME/WE.

POLITICAL STRINGS, CALL IT WHAT IT IS (THE ROOT).

WALKING.

WORK TOGETHER.

This, now we know, is the great deception: mankind created an idol god for you to idolize—an idol god, and religion to divide and conquer you, the human, You who are endowed with all the good power, not god power good energy.

"Not god power, good energy. This deception stripped you of the knowledge of the power you are."

Through this, divided and conquered, and to this day,

they have made you into slaves to them and enemies to yourselves and each other by the categorizations you allow and accept that they place upon you.

What makes you human is your humanity. You Know them by their LOVE (humanity)

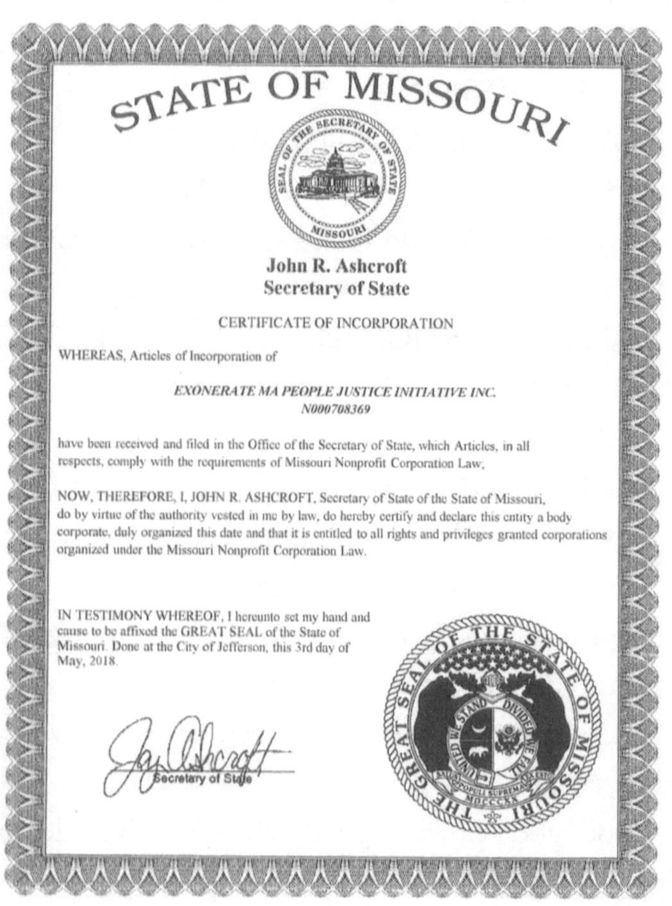

DOING YOUR THANG!

DOING YOUR THANG "Time Out for the Haters"

EMANCIPATE YOURSSELVES FROM
*   MENTAL SLAVERY*
NO MATTER WHAT THE CRISIS IS.
DOING, YA, DOING YA THANG.
IN THIS AGE OF TECHNOLOGICAL
*   INHUMANITY,*
SCIENTIFIC ATTROSITIES, ATOMIC
*   MISPHYLOSIPHIES, NUCLEAR*
MISENERGY, ITS A WORLD THAT
*   FORCES LIFELONG INSECURI-*
*   TIES (H.I.M)*
NO MATTER WHAT THE CRISIS IS
TIME OUT FOR THE HATERS,

THE TRADERS OF LOVE AND LIFE,
TRADING LOVE PASSION FOR
     VIOLENCE AND STRIFE
CAN'T EVEN HUG ONE ANOTHER
     GOT TO WRESTLE AND FIGHT
BABY GIVE ME A HUG
AFFECTION IS HIDDEN IN THE
     DARK LATE AT NIGHT
TIME OUT FOR THE HATERS THE
     TRADERS OF LOVE AND A
     HAPPY LIFE
WE GONNA CHAT DOWN
     HATERISM WITH ALL OUR
     MIGHT!
COME WE GO CHANT DOWN
     BABYLON ONE MORE TIME
ITS INSIGHT! LOVE GAVE US LIFE
     AND A HEART TO MAKE IT
     RIGHT
TIME OUT FOR THE HATERS THE
     FAKERS, LIARS, AND THE
     CHEATS,
YOU CAN NEVER COMPETE WITH
     LOVE PASSION, HATERS ARE
     OUT OF FASHION,
JEALOUSY, ENVY, VENGENCE,
     SPITE, ARROGANCE, IGNO-

RANCE, THE POMPUS VULGER
VIOLENT STENCH
ALL WRITTEN IN YOUR SCRIPT
FROM WILYE LYNCH,
LET IT GO! LET IT GO!
YOU OPEN YOUR EYES AND SEE
YOU'RE ACTING OUT, WHAT
SOME ONE TOLD YOU TO BE.
CULTURES AND COLORS STILL
PITTED AGAINST EACH OTHER
RACIALLY,
TIME OUT FOR THE HATERS, TOP
TRADERS OF LOVE AND A
HAPPY LIFE,
REMEMBERING HONOR RESPECT
AND UNITY WILL SHOW US
HOW TO LIVE FREE,
RESPECTING YOU RESPECTING
WE AND ALL HUMANS RESPEC-
TIVELY! DOING YA THANG!
THIS TREND WE BEGAN LOVING
US, YOU, WE, I AND I THE TREE
OF LOVE FOR HUMANITY,
CLOSING THE DOOR ON WAR
AND WORDS OF MASS
DESTRUCTION, PUT DOWN
THE GUNS!

LOVE UNDER CONSTRUCTION!
GET RID OF THE BOMBS,
WEAPSON NEED TO DISOLVE,
TAKE THE GUN POWDER OUT
OF POW, TAKE THE B OUT OF
BOMB, TAKE THE M ADD CAL
AND YOU HAVE CALM, THE
WORLD WITH NO BOMBS THE
WORLD WOULD BE CALM!
ELIMINATE THE THREAT! GET A
PET, AND RESET YOUR LIFE TO
LOVE NOT REGRET, TIME OUT
FOR THE HATERS THE INSTI-
GATERS OF PAIN CHAOS AND
DEATH! ITS TIME YOU GIVE IT
A REST! THE HATERS ARE
DISMISSED!
DISMISSED!!!!!
TIME OUT FOR THE HATERS,
TRADERS OF LOVE AND LIFE!
DOING YA THANG!

— :Rhonda-marie:Baker –EL ALL
RIGHTS RESERVED

SO PROUD TO FINALLY KNOW MY NATION-
ALITY DO YOU KNOW YOURS?

. . .

I AM Moorish American
  (Moorish American, Moroccan Empire)
  Priestess SahjKaya -EL

DECLARATION OF NATIONALITY
for Washitaw Muurs

I, ___________________, declare that I am a free and sovereign individual of this land of the ancient mound builders, known by it's indigenous name, Empire Washitaw de Dugdahmoundyah. I willingly and knowingly exercise my right to a nationality as a member of the indigenous Emperial Washitaw Nation of the Empire Washitaw de Dugdahmoundyah. I further reserve all of the fundamental freedoms and God-given rights of every human being upon this earth. Any and all, past and present political affiliations implied by operation of law or otherwise with foreign entities are hereby, now and forever, dissolved and revoked. Signed and witnessed this _____ day of the _______ month of the year _______.

[L.S.] X _____________________________
Bona Fide Signature

____
(Print Name)

____
Witness Bona Fide Signature

____
Witness Bona Fide Signature

____
Print Witness Name

____
Print Witness Name

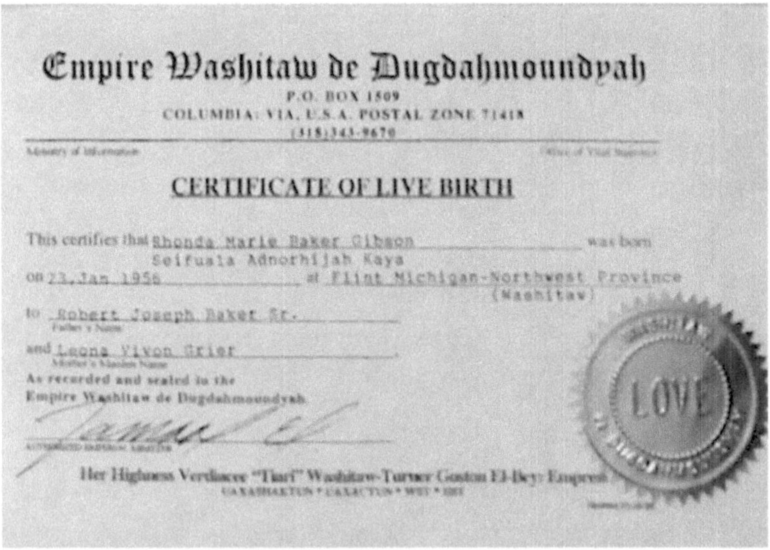

Empire Washitaw de Dugdahmoundyah

P.O. BOX 1509
COLUMBIA: VIA, U.S.A. POSTAL ZONE 71418
(318)343-9670

Ministry of Information   Office of Vital Statistics

CERTIFICATE OF LIVE BIRTH

This certifies that Rhonda Marie Baker Gibson   was born
Seifuala Adnorhijah Kaya

on 23 Jan 1956   at Flint Michigan-Northwest Province
(Washitaw)

to Robert Joseph Baker Sr.
Father's Name

and Leona Vivon Grier
Mother's Maiden Name

As recorded and sealed in the
Empire Washitaw de Dugdahmoundyah

AUTHORIZED SIGNING MINISTER

Her Highness Verdiacee "Tiari" Washitaw-Turner Goston El-Bey; Empress
UAXASHAKTUN * UAXACTUN * WET * EET